Madrid

Text: Pablo Caballero

EDICIONES
Aldeasa

Madrid

◄   *Puerta de Alcalá.*

Madrid the open city

Over the centuries, Madrid has always been a city that welcomed people from all over Spain. Today, it also welcomes people from all the corners of the world. Its mixed identity has been formed with the total of all these accents, customs and identities. This is probably why it is so easy to feel a part of the city as soon as you arrive.

Calle de Alcalá. ▶

Madrid is a modern, dynamic, open and cosmopolitan city. Its turbulent history has been closely linked to that of the Spanish Crown since the Court was moved there in 1561. It possesses a spectacular artistic and monumental legacy. It offers the visitor places as spectacular as the Palacio Real, Plaza Mayor or the Parque del Retiro. The artistic richness of the Prado, Reina Sofía Art Centre and Thyssen-Bornemisza museums, the three grand museums located on the Paseo del Prado, make Madrid one of the unmistakable reference points for all art lovers Without doubt, it is well worth visiting this grand city in which modernity and tradition are fused together, getting yourself lost in the dense layout of its streets and squares, enjoying its historical and cultural legacy, and of its current dynamism: and sharing the hospitality, spontaneity and particular way of understanding life of its inhabitants.

Witness to history

The first historical mention of Madrid dates back to the period of Muslim domination. At the end of the 9th century the Cordovan Emir Mohammed I built a defensive fortress on a hill alongside the River Manzanares. Around this forti-

Cathedral of Santa María la Real de la Almudena from Las Vistillas (above). ▲
Crystal Palace in the Parque del Retiro (below).
Plaza Mayor. Equestrian statue of Philip III. ▶

Hermitage of the Virgin of Puerto. ▲

Cathedral of the Almudena. Main façade. ▶

fication sprouted a small town known as Mayrit, which the Christians later called Magerit. After Alfonso VI of Castile conquered Toledo (1083-1085), the young city passed into the hands of the Christians without a struggle.

Throughout the 12th century Madrid consolidated its importance as a Castilian villa, or town. A new wall was built and the area covered nearly 33 hectares. Its privileges were confirmed during the reigns of Alfonso VII and Alfonso VIII, first with the awarding of the "Letter of Granting" and later, with the "City Charter". As the situation gradually stabilised over the rest of the Peninsula, the city took on more importance due to its strategic position on the communication routes between the northern and southern sub-plateaus. As from 1348 it obtained the privilege of being one of the twenty-four cities represented in the Courts of Castile. The population of Madrid gradually grew until reaching 5,000 inhabitants at the end of the 15th century.

The most significant event in the history of the city took place in 1561, when Philip II decided to move the Court from Toledo to Madrid. The event turned the city into the political centre of the Spanish monarchy. As a result, the population began to grow quickly. Substantial changes also took place in its appearance and social structure. Buildings

Puerta de Alcalá. ▲

Palacio de Comunicaciones. New City Council. ▶

owned by the nobility, churches and convents began to appear in the city, in line with its new status as home of the Court. In this period Madrid experienced one of the moments of great cultural splendour in the history of Spain. It was what is called the Golden Century. In a short space of time the city saw figures of the category and talents of Cervantes, Quevedo, Lope de Vega, Góngora, Calderón, Tirso de Molina, Velasquez, Alonso Cano, Rubens and Gómez de Mora, among others, coincide.

The arrival to the throne of Phillip V in 1700 represented the establishment of the Bourbon dynasty. Madrid continued to be a poor city without hygiene, disordered and lacking infrastructures. A series of important urban interventions were undertaken as an attempt to stop this situation. After the fire of the old royal palace, in 1734, works began on the construction of a new Palacio Real. The work took place between 1734 and 1764 under the direction of the architect Juan Bautista Sachetti.

Charles III was perhaps the monarch who did most to develop the city. He was responsible for interventions as important as the creation of public lighting and sewage systems, pavements and ornamentation in many streets, and the construction of cemeteries on the outskirts of the city.

He also made a decisive contribution to the monumental richness of the city.

The popular uprising of the 2nd of May 1808 against the Napoleonic troops and its subsequent repression are without doubts two of the most traumatic events in the history of the city. This event sparked the beginning of the War of Independence (1808-1814). Francisco de Goya was the artist who best expressed these tragic events in immortal works such as *The Shootings of May 3rd 1808, The Charge of the Mamelukes* or the series of *The Disasters of War*.

Joseph Bonaparte I applied a reformist programme during his short reign. He ordered the demolition of many houses, churches and convents in order to decongest the chaotic city centre. Thus appeared the public squares of Oriente, Santa Ana or Plaza de Ramales. For this reason he was popularly known as "Pepe Plazuelas" (Joe Squares).

After the Restoration, despite the absolutist death throes of Ferdinand VII, the new liberal and bourgeois ideas that came from Europe were now irremediably present. The romantic Madrid arose, in which cafés and theatres sprung up all over, often convulsed by the frequent revolutionary outbreaks and military revolts. Two decisive events contributed to changing the appearance of the city: the knocking-down of the wall of Phillip IV and the demolition of the many churches and convents as a result of the Mendizábal's Disentailment. This period also saw work beginning on the construction of the new districts extending the city. In the second half of the 19th century some large-scale infrastructures were undertaken, such as the Madrid-Aranjuez railway line (1851), or the Isabel II Canal, which enabled the city to be supplied by water.

At the beginning of the 20th century the population of Madrid reached 900,000 inhabitants. The city was expanding and absorbing nearby towns such as Carabancheles, Chamartín, Vallecas, Canillejas or Vicálvaro. They were turbulent times socially. Two anarchist bombs shook the Madrid society of the time. In 1906 Mateo Morral threw a bomb camouflaged as a bouquet of flowers at the royal procession after the wedding of Alfonso XIII and Victoria Eugenia de Battenberg. The monarchs were unharmed, but a terrible massacre occurred around the carriage. Six years later, another anarchist, Manuel Pardiñas, killed the President of the Government, José Canalejas, with two shots in front of the San Martín bookshop, in the Puerta del Sol, committing suicide afterwards.

Despite everything, Madrid gradually became a cosmopolitan city on a par with the big European capitals. The

Plaza de España. Monument to Cervantes (above). ▲
District of Las Letras (below).
Teatro Español at Plaza de Santa Ana (above). ▶
Templo de Debod at Parque del Oeste (below).

Nuevos Ministerios. Sculpture by Fernando Botero. ▲

Nuevos Ministerios and Azca. ▶

construction of Gran Vía, one of the most emblematic thoroughfares of the city centre, is the intervention that best represents these decades of relative boom. In 1931, the people of Madrid greeted with joy the proclamation of the Second Republic, which would represent a great advance in the recognition of fundamental rights and freedom.

The Civil War, just like in the rest of Spain, had devastating effects on the city. The area of Argüelles and the University City were the setting for the bloody confrontations during the "Battle of Madrid".

After the disappearance of General Franco's dictatorship and the return of democracy, Madrid has become, in a short time, one of the most dynamic cities in Europe. It has transformed itself with great naturalness into a large contemporary and cosmopolitan city, without losing the essential traits of its identity.

Visiting Madrid is to delve into a beautiful, chaotic, hospitable, lively city that is full of history and culture, a city that offers a wide range of possibilities. There are many reasons for discovering Madrid. Just a few words of warning: it may be addictive.

Old Madrid

The labyrinth of narrow streets and squares that extend from Palacio Real to Plaza Mayor forms the original centre from which the city of Madrid was shaped. In this small area are concentrated some of the most beautiful and emblematic spots of the city, places as representative as Palacio Real, Plaza Mayor or Plaza de la Villa. This area, full of life and delightful corners, is still today the heart of the city. It is an excellent spot for approaching the history of Madrid and for feeling the pulse of the contemporary metropolis.

Posada del Peine. ▶

Palacio Real. Porcelain Hall. ▲
Plaza de Oriente and Palacio Real. ▶

Palacio Real

The Palacio Real is probable the most emblematic building of Madrid due to its beauty, symbolic value and eventful history. It stands on the same site as that of the old defensive Muslim fortress of the 9th century. After the conquest by Alfonso VI of Castile, this area became the Royal Palace of the Christian kings. Over the centuries it experienced many remodellings and enlargements, until Phillip II brought the Court here. A massive fire, that lasted three days, destroyed the Royal Palace on Christmas Eve 1734. Phillip V decided to build a new palace on the same site as a symbol of the continuity of the Spanish monarchy with the House of Bourbon. The first project was entrusted to the architect Filippo Juvara, who after his death in 1736 was replaced by his pupil Juan Bautista Sachetti, who completely amended the original design. Alongside him worked other leading architects such as Ventura Rodríguez and Francesco Sabatini.

Work began on the 6th of April 1738 and continued until 1764. Sachetti designed a ground plan that conserved the traditional Spanish form of rectangular central courtyard, adding some strong projections in the corners as a reminder

of the towers of the old Royal Palace. The façades, built with granite and white Colmenar stone for the relief work and details, were inspired by those produced by Bernini for the Louvre. The elevation of the palaces comprises two sections: a dressed stone base and an upper body of Ionic order with gigantic pilasters, crowned by cornice and balustrade. Facing the main façade extends the esplanade of the Plaza de Armas, similar to that of the burnt-down Royal Palace. During the reign of Ferdinand VI the works were speeded up until completing the whole exterior.

Charles III was the first monarch to inhabit it, on the 1st of December 1764. Rich materials were used for the interior decoration: marbles, stuccos, mahogany, etc. Also involved were the most famous European painters of the time. Thus in the different rooms we can see the fresco paintings of Rafael Mengs, Juan Bautista Tiépolo and Corrado Giaquinto. The decoration of the Palacio Real has been changed according to the different artistic styles of each prior and depending on the tastes of the successive monarchs. From the period of Charles III are conserved the Throne Room, the Kings' Chamber and the Porcelain Room; from the kingdom of Charles IV the Hall of Mirrors stands out, and from the time of Alfonso XII the Gala Dining Room. The magnificent

Cathedral of Santa María la Real de la Almudena (above). ▼
Teatro Real in the Plaza de Isabel II (below).
Plaza de Oriente and back façade of the Teatro Real. ▶

chapel, work of Ventura Rodríguez and Sachetti, is one of the most beautiful parts of the complex.

The Palacio Real houses an enormous artistic richness, with works by Goya, Velasquez, El Greco, Rubens, Caravaggio, Bernini and Cellini, among many others. Moreover, it has an extremely valuable collection of decorative arts that includes magnificent porcelains, watches, tapestries and items of furniture. The Royal Pharmacy and Royal Armoury are also very interesting collections.

The gardens surrounding the building are from later periods. The Sabatini Gardens, situated in the north part, were built in the thirties and are of French design. What is called the Campo del Moro is reached along Paseo de la Virgen del Puerto. From here one gets a marvellous view of the later façade of the palace. They were created in the time of Isabel II, following the design of the 19th-century English parks.

Plaza Mayor

This magnificent arcaded square is one of the most beautiful, liveliest and important spots in Madrid. The history of this space dates back to 1581, when Phillip II decided to transform the old Plaza del Arrabal, where the mar-

Sabatini Gardens with the Palacio Real (above). ▲
A peacock in the gardens of the Campo del Moro (below).
Plaza Mayor. Arco de Cuchilleros. ▶

ket was held, into a large space that could hold solemn and popular acts. The initial head of the project was the architect Juan de Herrera. However, it was Juan Gómez de Mora who completed the new square in 1619. The area immediately became the centre of the city's public life.

Plaza Mayor has suffered several fires that have altered its original appearance. The 1790 fire was particularly devastating. During the reconstruction undertaken by Juan de Villanueva the appearance of the square was notably modified, the height of the surrounding houses being lowered from five to three storeys and entrance arches built in the corners.

The square is rectangular in shape, measuring 129 m by 94 m. It has nine entrance gates, the Arco de Cuchilleros being the most outstanding of them. The north side features the Casa de la Panadería, which was originally the main bakery of the old Villa. The fresco paintings of the façade really attract one's attention, produced by Carlos Franco in 1992. On the opposite side is what is called Casa de la Carnicería. The equestrian statue of Phillip III that stands in the centre of the square was produced by the Italians Juan de Bolonia and Pietro Tacca in 1616.

Plaza Mayor. Philately and coin collecting market. ▲

Plaza Mayor. Statue of Philip III and the Casa de la Panadería. ▶

Plaza Mayor has always been a massively important setting for the public life of the city. All kinds of events and celebrations have been held here over the centuries. It has been witness to royal celebrations and festivities, religious celebrations of all kinds, popular festivals, markets, carnivals, representations of eucharistic plays, bullfights and even executions. As well as its obvious historical and monumental interest, Plaza Mayor is still one of the city's main epicentres, although, to a lesser extent, it still hosts a fair number of events every year, mainly musical performances and diverse fairs. In its arcades and neighbouring streets are concentrated a large proportion of the more traditional shops. Sunday mornings the arcades are reserved for a popular stamp-collecting and coin-collecting market.

Very close by, in Plaza de la Provincia, is another magnificent building that is well worth visiting. It is the Palacio de Santa Cruz, current home of the Ministry of Foreign Affairs. It was built between 1629 and 1636, according to the design of Juan Gómez de Mora, the works being led by Cristóbal Aguilera. Its original function was to house the rooms of the Mayors' Hall and the Court prison.

Fresco paintings of the Casa de la Panadería by Carlos Franco (above). ▲
Church tower of San Ginés (below).
Calle del Arenal (above). ▶
Pasadizo de San Ginés (below).

Plaza de la Villa. Old City Council. ▲

Plaza de la Villa. Lujanes Tower. ▶

Plaza de la Villa

Plaza de la Villa is one of the most beautiful and welcoming corners of the city. It is situated alongside Calle Mayor, very close therefore to the Palacio Real and Plaza Mayor.

The small space is home to three highly valuable buildings. The first one starting on the left is the house-tower of Los Lujanes, one of the few examples of 15th-century architecture conserved in the city. The tower, in masonry and brick, is the oldest part of the whole building. It features the beautiful horseshoe arch that leads to Calle del Codo. Some of its most outstanding elements are the Gothic doorway and the heraldic coats of arms. Today it is the home of the Royal Academy of Moral and Political Sciences.

At the end of the square is Casa de Cisneros, an impressive palatial house in Plateresque style built in 1537 by Benito Jiménez de Cisneros, nephew of the famous cardinal. The façade facing Calle del Sacramento is the most outstanding part of the original building. The façade facing Plaza de la Villa and the projecting balcony that connects with the old City Hall forms part of the restructuring undertaken by Luis Bellido at the beginning of the 20th century.

On the right of the square is Casa de la Villa, home of Madrid City Council. Work started on the building in 1644 according to the project of Juan Gómez de Mora, who was succeeded in 1648 by his pupil José Villarreal. Teodoro Ardemans and José del Olmo produced the two doorways of the main façade. The two large slate-roofed towers at the ends give the building an air of solemnity. Of the later reforms we should mention that produced by Juan de Villanueva in 1789, who added the gallery facing Calle Mayor. The Council Chamber, the stone stairway, the Goya Hall and the old chapel are some of the most beautiful rooms inside.

The statue in the centre of the square is dedicated to Álvaro de Bazán, hero of the Battle of Lepanto, and is the work of Mariano Benlliure.

Monastery of the Descalzas Reales

The monastery of the Descalzas Reales is situated in the square of the same name, close to Calle del Arenal and the Puerta del Sol. It occupies and old palace in which Charles I and Isabel of Portugal lived. The convent was founded by their daughter, Juana, in 1557. The most out-

Casa Labra. ▲

Monastery of the Descalzas Reales. ▶

standing part of the series of buildings is the church, built over a single nave with barrel vaulting. The project was headed by the architect Antonio Sillero, while the delightful Renaissance doorway of the church is the work of Juan Bautista de Toledo. The rows of seats of the altar, choir and sacristy were produced by Juan Gómez de Mora in 1612. The part of the monastery that can be visited contains an impressive art collection with works by painters of the category of Zurbarán, Claudio Coello, Titian and Rubens.

Monastery of the Encarnación

Quite close, next to the Palacio del Senado, is another remarkable Madrid monastery, that of the Encarnación, founded in 1611 by Phillip III and Margaret of Austria. The building is the work of the architects Juan Gómez de Mora and Friar Alberto de la Madre de Dios. It was the first of the long series of convents built in Madrid during the 17th century. The façade, built in granite, comprises an entrance portico with three arches, over which stands a second section with windows, two royal coats of arms and a bas-relief by Antonio de Riera that represents *The Annunciation*. Of note is the church built over a Latin cross ground plan, with cross-aisle and dome. In 1761, after a fire, Ventura Rodríguez remodelled its interior in neo-classical style.

The convent conserves an important pictorial and sculptural legacy from the 17th and 18th centuries, with works by Lucas Jordán, Juan van der Hammen, Vicente Carducho, Gregorio Fernández and Pedro de Mena. Also of great interest is the reliquary, made up of more than seven hundred items produced in different materials from Italy, Germany, Spain and the Low Countries.

Calle de Bailén. Wafer seller (above). ▸
Palacio del Senado (below).
Monastery of the Encarnación. ▸

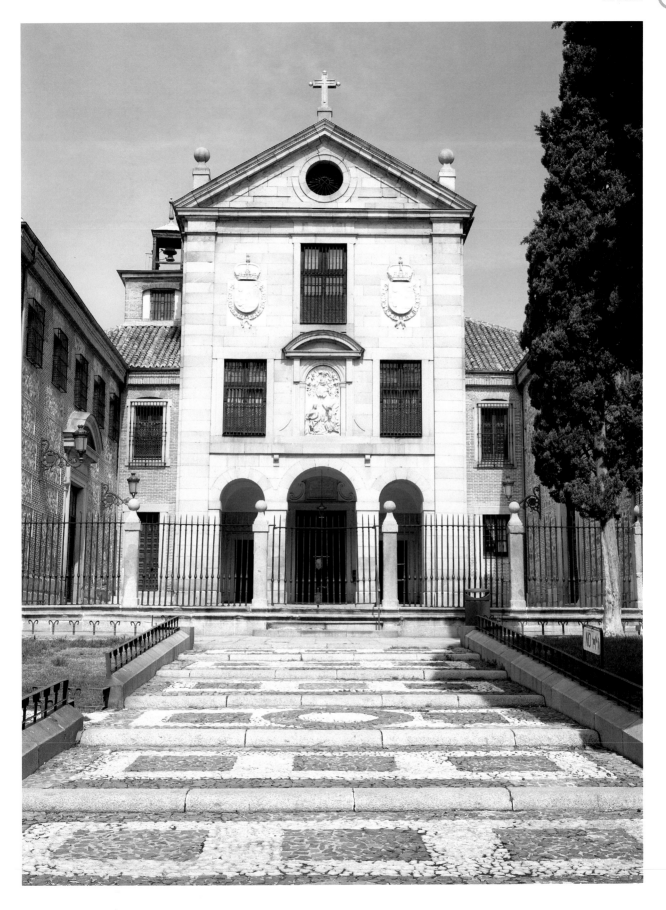

Paseo del Prado, Paseo de Recoletos and Paseo de la Castellana

Paseo del Prado, Paseo de Recoletos and Paseo de la Castellana form an axis that divides the city from north to south. Along these three key thoroughfares are the majority of the most important museums, cultural institutions, official entities and business centres in the city. Walking along these wide avenues is to follow the evolution of Madrid from the mid-18th century to the present.

It is difficult to find a street anywhere in the world with a concentration of masterpieces of the history of painting similar to that of Paseo del Prado. The Prado National Museum, the Reina National Museum Art Centre and the Thyssen-Bornemisza Museum are a powerful attraction that no art lover should miss.

Fountain of Neptuno. ▶

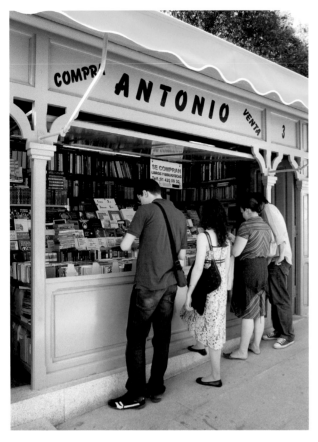

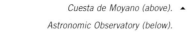

Cuesta de Moyano (above). ▲
Astronomic Observatory (below).
Tropical gardens at the old Atocha Station. ▶

Reina Sofía National Museum Art Centre

The Reina Sofía is at the end of Calle de Santa Isabel, almost opposite Atocha Station. Its collection is dedicated to contemporary art and brings together artists of the category of Salvador Dalí, Picasso, Joan Miró, Juan Gris, Kandinsky, Francis Bacon, Eduardo Chillida and Antonio Tàpies, among many others. However, probably the main reason why it is known the world over is because the Pablo Picasso's famous *Guernica* is on show there, one of the most famous works by the brilliant Malaga painter.

The museum occupies the building of the old hospital of San Carlos, the origins of which date back to 1566. In the second half of the 18th century, Charles III entrusted Francesco Sabatini with the construction of a new hospital over an earlier design by Hermosilla.

After years of abandon, the building was declared a Historical-Artistic Monument in 1977. In 1980 the restoration and remodelling of the property began under the direction of Antonio Fernández Alba. At the end of 1988 José Luis Íñiguez de Onzoño and Antonio Vázquez de Castro made the final modifications. The transparent lifts situated on the main entrance and produced in cooperation with the

Guernica by Picasso (above). ▲
Enlargement by Jean Nouvel (below).
Sabatini building's entrance. ▶

British Ian Ritchie, are perhaps the most attractive element of this latest intervention. In 1988 it was officially opened, mainly to hold temporary exhibitions. The new museum, which incorporated the collections of the former Spanish Museum of Contemporary Art, was opened in 1992. The recent enlargement completed in 2005 doubles the space of the museum and greatly improves its facilities. It was produced by the leading architect Jean Nouvel.

The Palacio de Velázquez and the Palacio de Cristal, situated in the Parque del Retiro, depend on the museum and house temporary exhibitions.

Prado National Museum

Madrid has a great many attractions and plenty to please everyone who visits it. The Prado Museum is undoubtedly one of the great jewels of the city and perhaps its greatest attraction internationally. This fame is more than justified since we find ourselves before one of the best art collections in the world, an essential reference point of Spanish culture.

The quantity (8,600 works) and the quality of the paintings that the Prado possesses has partly eclipsed the impor-

Prado Museum. The Clothed Maja by Goya (above). ▲
Goya Doorway (below).
Velázquez Doorway (above). ▶
Murillo Doorway (below).

tance of the other collections, such as the drawings and engravings, that of the coins and medals or what is called the Dauphin's Treasure.

The Prado Museum has undergone several remodellings throughout its history. The most recent, of great magnitude, was designed by the architect Rafael Moneo and has increased the museum space by 22,000 m². Of note here are the entrance doors of the enlargement by the sculptress Cristina Iglesias. Also agreed is the transfer of the Kings Hall (former Army Museum) to the museum.

The works on show range from 12th-century murals through to Goya (19th century). The best-represented schools are the Spanish, Flemish and Italian. El Greco, Velasquez, Goya, Rubens, Van Dyck, Brueghel, Fra Angelico, Titian, Caravaggio; the list of grand masters whose works we can see in the Prado Museum is unending, impossible to cover in just one visit. There are also excellent collections, although less in number, of French and German painting. Visiting this exceptional museum is an unforgettable experience for seasoned art lovers and the uninitiated alike.

The building was initially planned within the enlightened reforms of Charles III, such as the Natural History Museum. The architect entrusted with the works was Juan de Villanueva, who designed a lengthened construction following the axis of a well-lit gallery crowned and divided in the centre by three larger sections: two cubes at the ends and a building with a basilica ground plan in the centre. The result is one of the summits of Spanish neo-classicism. During the War of Independence it was used as an arsenal and barracks for the cavalry of the Napoleonic armies, and was seriously damaged by such use. On the 19th of November 1819, by this time during the reign of Ferdinand VII, it was finally opened with the name of the Royal Museum of Paintings.

The most attractive part of the exterior decoration is the large frieze over the doorway by Velasquez, which leads to Paseo del Prado. It shows an allegory of King Ferdinand VII as protector of the sciences, arts and technology; behind the king figures appear of various mythological gods. In the decoration of the façade one can also observe the busts of some of the most outstanding Spanish artists.

Thyssen-Bornemisza Museum

On the corner between Paseo del Prado and Carrera de San Jerónimo is the third side of this spectacular triangle of art, the Thyssen-Bornemisza Museum. Its magnificent

Casón del Buen Retiro seen from the Parque del Retiro (above). ▲
Detail of the new building of the Prado Museum (below).
Detail of the doors by the sculptress Cristina Iglesias. ▶

Paseo del Prado. Fountain of Apolo. ▲

Plaza de Cánovas del Castillo. Fountain of Neptuno. ▶

collection complements those of the Prado and Reina Sofía museums to perfection, since it adds excellent examples of different styles and schools. It exhibits masterpieces of the early Italian and Dutch painters, of the German Renaissance, 17th-century Dutch painting, impressionism, German expressionism, Russian constructivism, geometric abstraction and pop art. The museum houses what was without doubt one of the most important private collections in the world, that of Baron Hans Heinrich Thyssen-Bornemisza. After an agreement between the Spanish State and the Baron, the museum was opened in 1992. One year later the collection was definitively acquired by the Spanish State.

Visiting the Thyssen Museum is taking a tour through the history of European painting from the 13th to the 20th century. Among the nearly one thousand works on show one can see paintings by El Greco, Titian, Tintoretto, Caravaggio, Albert Dürer, Lucas Cranach, Rubens, Van Gogh, Gauguin, Picasso, Mondrian, Marc Chagall, Klee, Edward Hopper and Richard Estes: a gathering of impressive masterpieces.

The museum occupies the rooms of the Palacio de Villahermosa, an elegant neo-classical building dating from the late-18th and early-19th centuries, following the project of Antonio López Aguado. The rehabilitation and enlargement of the property to turn it into a museum was entrusted to the architect Rafael Moneo. The last remodelling work took place in 2004. After the purchase of neighbouring properties, restoration work began on the new building by the architects Manuel Baquero and Francesc Pla. These new spaces house the items from the Carmen Thyssen-Bornemisza collection that include excellent examples of 17th-century Dutch painting, French and North American naturalist landscape painting, impressionism, post-impressionism and early 20th-century vanguard art.

Paseo de Recoletos

Paseo de Recoletos runs between Plaza de Cibeles and Plaza de Colón. This pleasant tree-lined avenue, with its wide central boulevard, from its remodelling in the 19th century, became the residence of some of the wealthiest families in the city. All along it there are points of great interest. Starting from Cibeles, at number 10 is the palace of the Marquis of Salamanca, an excellent example of 19th-century palatial architecture. It was built by Narciso Tomás y Colomer between 1845 and 1855.

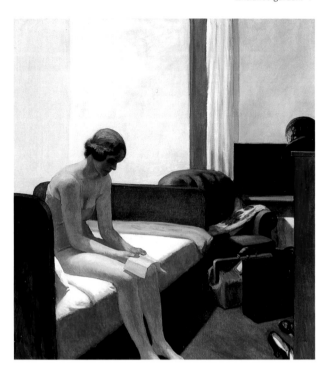

Thyssen-Bornemisza Museum.
Stanza d'albergo, by Edward Hopper (above). ▾
Rooms of the enlargement (below).
Entrance garden. ▸

The Café de Gijón, at number 21, is one of the most traditional establishments in Madrid. It was opened in 1888 and after the Civil War it became one of the favourite spots for the city's artists and intellectuals. Its famous informal gatherings have attracted such illustrious figures as Ramón y Cajal, Buero Vallejo, Gerardo Diego, Camilo José Cela and Fernando Fernán Gómez, among many others.

Next to Plaza de Colón a massive neoclassical building stands out. It was designed by Francisco Jareño and was completed in 1892. Today it is the home of two important institutions: the National Library, with its extremely valuable bibliographical archive of 17 million documents that include manuscripts, incunabula, engravings, drawings, maps, scores and photographs, and the National Archaeological Museum, with an interesting collection of archaeological objects that provide an overview of the history of the Iberian Peninsula from prehistoric times through to the 19th century (it is on the side that leads to Calle de Serrano). Its most famous piece is probably the *Lady of Elche*, a peak in Iberian art. In the museum's garden there is a reproduction of the prehistoric caves of Altamira.

Paseo de Recoletos (above). ▲
Café de Gijón (below).
National Library. ▶

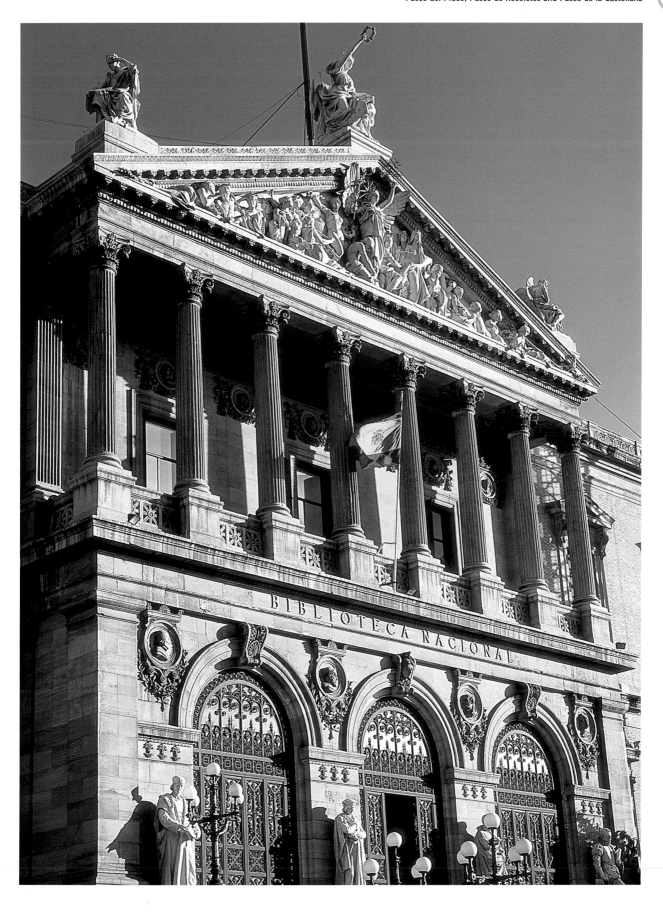

Plaza de Colón

Plaza de Colón marks the end of Paseo del Prado and the beginning of Paseo de la Castellana. The Gardens of the Discovery occupy the entire east-facing side. Here stands the monument to Columbus. Produced in neo-Gothic style, it is the work of the sculptors Jerónimo Suñol and Arturo Mélida and was made between 1881 and 1885.

On the opposite side feature the spectacular Torres Colón towers with their characteristic deep red glass façades. They were built in 1976 under the direction of Antonio Lamela, a clear sign that we are entering into the financial heart of contemporary Madrid.

Also in the square is the Wax Museum that exhibits more than 500 representations of historical and famous personalities.

District of Salamanca

The district of Salamanca is the area between Paseo de la Castellana and Calle de Alcalá, Calle Francisco Silvela and Calle María de Molina. It was built at the end of the 19th century, during the Restoration, and is one of the most dis-

Plaza de Colón. Gardens of Discovery (above). ▲
Plaza de Colón. Monument to Columbus (below).
National Archaeological Museum. ▶

tinguished and commercial areas of the city. In its wide streets in the form of a grid are some of the most luxurious and exclusive shops and boutiques in Madrid. Calle de Serrano, full of luxury outlets, is possibly one of the streets that best represents this exclusive district. At number 61 is the "ABC Serrano" shopping centre, installed in a beautiful building dating 1899 under the direction of José López Sallaberry, and enlarged in 1926 by the architect Aníbal González. It was originally the offices of the *ABC* newspaper and *Blanco y Negro* magazine.

At number 22 of the same street is the Lázaro Galdiano Museum. Its rooms house works of art and diverse objects that belonged to the private collection of the financier José Lázaro Galdiano (1862-1947). The majority of the pieces are dedicated to the decorative arts. Its magnificent painting collection includes works by Zurbarán, Goya and El Greco. The Fundación Juan March, at number 77 Calle Castelló, regularly organises excellent exhibitions and all kinds of cultural events.

"ABC Serrano" commercial centre (above). ▼
Lázaro Galdiano Museum (below).
Fundación Juan March (above). ▶
Paseo de la Castellana (below).

Paseo de la Castellana

Cuatro Torres Business Area. ▶
Sorolla Museum (above). ▼
Plaza de Emilio Castelar (below).

Paseo de la Castellana is the financial centre of the city. Many big companies have their head offices here. Walking along it is like a journey through the architecture of Madrid from the 20th century to the modernity of the present. On this route one can see magnificent buildings, such as the Bankinter building (1976) at number 29. Another interesting point is the Azca business complex, which has some of the tallest skyscrapers on the avenue. Here stands the BBVA building (1979-1980), designed by Javier Sáenz de Oiza and the Torre Picasso, by Minoru Yamasaki. Very close, in Plaza de Lima, is the Torre Europa (1985), designed by Miguel Oriol e Ybarra. In Plaza de Castilla is the famous Puerta Europa with its leaning towers.

You should visit number 37 of the nearby Calle del General Martínez Campos the Sorolla Museum, located in the house-studio of the great Valencia artist. Nearly at the same level as the Nuevos Ministerios building is another museum, the Natural Science Museum. The construction of the Cuatro Torres Business Area, to the north of Plaza de Castilla, will revolutionise the skyline of Paseo de la Castellana. The four skyscrapers will easily surpass 200 m.

Puerta del Sol, Calles de Alcalá and Gran Vía

The Puerta del Sol is the essential reference point of the city centre, an almost mandatory stopping-off point every day for thousands of Madrid locals and visitors. Since its creation it has been witness to a good many of the events that have marked the history of Madrid. Calle de Alcalá and Gran Vía are the two main thoroughfares that divide and shape all this central area. They are the two emblematic avenues that untangle the dense centre of the city. They comprise a wonderful example of its evolution from the 18th century until the mid-20th century. As well as the beauty and importance of some of its buildings and monuments, these two busy streets are an ideal place to feel the day-to-day heartbeat of the city. Walking along their always-packed pavements, surrounded by people from all over the world, is an excellent way of getting to know contemporary Madrid.

Metrópolis building at the junction of Calles de Alcalá and Gran Vía. ▶

Puerta del Sol metro station. ▲

Plaza de Canalejas. ▶

Puerta del Sol

This semicircular-shaped public square is one of the most famous and busiest in Madrid. When someone mentions the city centre, they are probably thinking of the Puerta del Sol. This is where kilometre 0 of the Spanish road system radiates out from. It is undoubtedly one of the nerve centres and key communication points of the city, and the setting for some of the most important events of the last three centuries. It bore witness, for example, to the Esquilache riot in 1766, the poplar uprising against the Napoleonic troops on the 2nd of May 1808, or the reading of the Constitution of Cádiz and the proclamation of Ferdinand VII as constitutional king in 1812. Here start some of the most important streets of the centre: Mayor, Arenal, Carrera de San Jerónimo or Alcalá.

The Puerta del Sol was one of the old entrances of the wall that surrounded the city in the 15th century. This wall separated the suburbs that had gradually grown outside the Christian wall of the 12th century. The construction of the Real Casa de Correos, designed by the French architect Jaime Marquet and built between 1766 and 1768, was the start of the current shape of the square. The building is

notable for its large horizontal façade which combines brickwork with Colmenar stone. The large stone doorway is crowned with a large triangular pediment that has the royal coat of arms, lions and trophies carved out of it. From 1847 the building housed the offices of the Ministry of Government. That was when they started to demolish several houses and convents to create a large square around the building. Today it houses the Presidency of the Community of Madrid and continues to be one of the most representative buildings of the city.

The clock tower, one of the outstanding elements of the property, was added in 1866. It is probably the most famous clock tower in Spain. Every 31st of December, as the clock strikes 12, millions of Spanish people welcome in the New Year eating twelve grapes to the sound of the chimes of the clock tower. On this night Puerta del Sol becomes the setting for a mass celebration.

The statue of the Bear and the Strawberry Tree, symbol of the city of Madrid, is one of the most outstanding ornamental aspects of the Puerta del Sol. It faces Calle del Carmen. The equestrian statue of Charles III that overlooks the square is a reproduction of the work by Juan de Mena that is kept in the Real Academia de Bellas Artes de San

Puerta del Sol. Kilometre Zero (above). ▲
Staue of Charles III (below).
Real Casa de Correos (above). ▶
"Tío Pepe" advertisement. Detail (below left).
Statue of the Bear and Strawberry Tree (below right).

Fernando. It was produced in 1994 by Miguel Ángel Rodríguez and Eduardo Zancada. Mention should also be made of the picturesque neon sign advertising "Tío Pepe" wines, so often portrayed by painters, photographers and filmmakers, turning it into an icon of the city.

Calle de Alcalá

Calle de Alcalá is one of the longest and oldest streets in Madrid. Along it, especially at the beginning, are some of the most emblematic buildings and monuments of the city. The Real Academia de Bellas Artes de San Fernando, Plaza de Cibeles or the extremely famous Puerta de Alcalá, are just some of the most outstanding examples of the richness and interest of the beautiful, long street.

Its origins date back to the 15th century. The layout corresponds to that of the old road that came from Puerta del Sol, at that time the city limits, and went towards Alcalá de Henares. This street quickly became one of the most important thoroughfares of Madrid. In the 17th century some of the most important palaces and convents of the city were to be found here. From this period is conserved one of the jewels of Madrid Baroque, the church of the Concepción Real de Calatrava, at number 25, which formed part of the now-disappeared royal monastery of the Concepción, and which was built between 1670 and 1678 by Friar Lorenzo de San Nicolás. Its interior features the altarpiece made by Churriguera for the main chapel.

In the 18th century, with the arrival of the Bourbon dynasty, new public buildings began to arise of an official and academic nature. For example, at number 9 is the Real Casa de Aduanas (Royal Customs House), currently the offices of the Treasury. This large neo-classical property was built between 1761 and 1769 at the behest of Charles III, following a design by Sabatini. Right beside it is the centre of the Real Academia de las Bellas Artes de San Fernando, built in 1724 by José Benito Churriguera as a palace for Juan de Goyeneche. Inside one can admire a magnificent collection of paintings with works by Goya, Zurbarán, Ribera, Rubens, Van Loo, Madrazo and Juan Gris.

Calle de Alcalá has always adapted its appearance to the spirit of changing times. Thus at the end of the 19th and beginning of the 20th centuries splendid bank buildings began to proliferate. The avenue became the nerve centre of the financial capital based in Madrid. In the section that runs between Puerta del Sol and Plaza de Cibeles one can see interesting buildings representative of this period. At number

Círculo de Bellas Artes (above). ▲
Royal Academy of Fine Arts of San Fernando (below).
Casino de Madrid. ▶

Dome of the Metrópolis building. ▲

Casa de las Siete Chimeneas. ▶

Placcque on the Banco Español de Crédito. ▲

Banco de Bilbao building. ▶

31 is what was the offices of the Banco Mercantil e Industrial, built between 1933 and 1945 by the architect Antonio Palacios, currently home to the Department of Culture and Sports of the Community of Madrid. A little further on we come to one of the most characteristic images of the city, the Metrópolis building, with its spectacular tower crowned by a formidable dome with scales, in turn crowned with a winged Victory. It was built between 1905 and 1911 by the French architects Jules and Raymond Février for the "La Unión y el Fénix" insurance company. Another excellent example of early 20th century architecture is the Banco del Río de la Plata, work of Antonio Palacios and Joaquín Otamendi, today the home of the Instituto Cervantes.

On the same stretch of street, on the side with the even numbers, there are also some fantastic buildings. At number 16 our attention is attracted by two monumental chariots in bronze that crown the towers of the Banco de Bilbao building, designed by the architect Ricardo Bastida y Bilbao and built between 1920 and 1923. At number 42 stands out the centre of the Círculo de Bellas Artes, opened in 1926, another of the jewels by the great architect Antonio Palacios built in Madrid. The Círculo de Bellas Artes continues to be one of the most active and interesting cultural institutions in the city.

Moving along Calle de Alcalá there are other emblematic points of Madrid such as Plaza de Cibeles and the Puerta de Alcalá. Also, although further from the centre, is the Las Ventas bullring. This bullring, in neo-Mudejar style, is one of the world's leading bullfighting centres with a capacity of 23,000 spectators. The main festival of the year is Saint Isidore, which is held in May.

Plaza de Cibeles

One of the unmistakable icons of the city is the Cibeles fountain that overlooks the square of the same name. It represents the Goddess Cybele, the goddess of the Earth, agriculture and fertility, on a chariot pulled by two lions. The fountain was built following a design by Ventura Rodríguez. The goddess and the lions were made in marble and the rest of the piece in Redueña stone. Different artists took part in its production. Francisco Gutiérrez was entrusted with the figure of the goddess and the chariot, the lions are the work of Roberto Michel and the adornments by Miguel Ximénez. The fountain was installed in 1782 alongside the Palacio de Buenavista, facing the Fountain of Neptuno. Its direction and location was later changed.

Palacio de Linares (above). ▲
Banco de España (below).
Fountain of Cibeles. ▶

Plaza de Cibeles is one of the most beautiful in the city. Four exceptional buildings border it and define this space. Going down from the Puerta del Sol, on the side with even numbers, the monumental building of the Banco de España stands out, work of the architects Eduardo Adaro and Severiano Sainz de Lastra. It was opened in 1891 and is one of the best examples of eclectic architecture. Its façades are decorated with a full repertoire of Renaissance elements. Just opposite we can admire another notable construction surrounded by a large garden. It is the Palacio de Buenavista, built in the late-18th century, and which today is the General Headquarters of the Land Army. On the opposite side of the square the imposing Palacio de Comunicaciones projects out, built by Antonio Palacios, Julián Otamendi and the engineer Ángel Chueca, between 1904 and 1917. This enormous spectacular building has become one of the most representative of the city. "Today the headquarters of Madrid City Council, it no longer houses the central offices of the Post Office." Facing it is the Palacio de Linares, work of the architect Carlos Coludí. It is a lovely 19th-century construction that today houses the Casa de América. This institution undertakes a large number of cultural activities throughout the year.

Puerta de Alcalá

In the Plaza de la Independencia, close to Cibeles and a short distance from the main entrance to the Parque del Retiro, is another of the most important and well-known monuments of Madrid, the Puerta de Alcalá. Charles III ordered it to be built to replace an earlier, highly deteriorated one, built in the times of Phillip IV. It opened in 1778 and is the work of Francesco Sabatini. It was not originally an ornamental element, but formed part of the wall that surrounded the city and which was not finally demolished until 1869.

The Puerta de Alcalá stands out for its balance and elegance. It has five openings, three of them with semicircular arches and the other two lintelled. In the attic of the central part one can read the following inscription: *Regge Carolo III. Anno MDCCLXXVIII*. Curiously it is written in Italian. It appears that Sabatini used his mother tongue instead of Latin or Spanish, and nobody noticed it. Over the inscription is the coat of arms held up by Fame and a spirit.

Puerta de Alcalá. ▶

Gran Vía

Gran Vía is one of the main thoroughfares of the city centre. This beautiful avenue, overflowing with life and activity at any time of day or night, is one of the streets that best define contemporary Madrid. It is a relatively new street, the works for its construction having started in 1910, although the first design produced by Carlos Velasco dates back to 1862. There was a pressing need to create a large avenue that connected the new districts, arising in the northeast, with the city centre and relieving the concentration of traffic in the Puerta del Sol. The undertaking of the project was delayed due to its complexity and magnitude. 334 buildings had to be demolished to carry out the works. Houses and churches disappeared in order to create this large avenue that immediately became one of the prides of the city.

Its layout comprises three clearly differentiated sections. The first one starts in Alcalá and goes as far as Calle de la Montera. It was built between 1910 and 1917. The second, built between 1917 and 1921, goes from this point as far as the Plaza del Callao. The works on the third part that leads to Plaza de España began in 1925.

Gran Vía is home to many offices, banks, shops, cinemas and theatres. Strolling along its pavements one can take in a great many magnificent buildings. At number 1 is the attractive Grassy building, built between 1916 and 1917 by the architect Eladio Laredo y Carranza. Its most outstanding element is the rotunda on the corner crowned by two superimposed niches of Renaissance influence. On the corner with Calle de Fuencarral stands the famous Telefónica building, one of the grand icons of the street. It was the first skyscraper in Madrid (1929). The project was entrusted to the North American architect Louis Weeks and the artistic decoration is the work of Ignacio de Cárdenas Pastor.

In Plaza del Callao there are other notable examples of 20th-century architecture. The Capitol building, with its spectacular form of an ocean liner and its rationalist air, is one of the most splendid buildings in Gran Vía. It was built by two young architects, Luis Martínez Feduchi and Vicente Eced y Eced. Just as notable is the Palacio de la Prensa, work of Pedro Muguruza Ontaño, which stands out for its large scale and monument-like air. The most attractive part is perhaps the front of the spectacular tower, which contains an extremely high triumphal arch.

Another point of Gran Vía where it is well worth stopping is the Museo Chicote, at number 12. It is one of the most traditional and prestigious bars in the city. The list of famous

Telefónica building (above). ▲
Capitol building. Luminous sign (below).
Gran Vía from the Plaza de España. ▶

people who have sipped their famous cocktails is endless. It was the favourite spot of North American film stars passing through the city. This bar has been able to adapt to new times and is still an excellent spot for making a stop-off on the route.

Plaza de España

Gran Vía leads to Plaza de España. Within the complex stands the monument to Miguel de Cervantes which over-looks the gardens adorning the square. Rafael Martínez Zapatero and Lorenzo Coullant won the tender put out for its construction to commemorate the third centenary of the death of the brilliant writer. The works began in 1928. At the base of then monument are the figures of Don Quixote and Sancho Panza, and above them sitting on a pedestal Miguel de Cervantes. The work was not completed until after the Civil War, under the direction of Coullant's son.

Two other outstanding buildings in the square deserve a special mention. The first of them is the España building, built between 1947 and 1953 under the direction of Julián and José María Otamendi, following the model of the North American skyscrapers. The façade is brick and limestone, and is decorated with a neo-Baroque doorway. The same

Plaza de Callao (above). ▲
Plaza de España (below).
Monument to Cervantes in the Plaza de España. ▶

Cerralbo Museum. ▲
Cuartel del Conde Duque. ▶

architects designed the Torre de Madrid (1954-57) which, with its 32 storeys and 130 metres' height, was conceived as the tallest concrete building in the world. It was also, until the construction of Torre España, the tallest building in Madrid.

The Maravillas district

This popular district is an active and lively area, full of small shops with a modern outlook and night spots. Its history, as the names of its streets and squares recall, is closely linked to the popular uprising of the 2nd of May 1808, which sparked off the War of Independence (1808-1814).

The old barracks of the Conde Duque, in the street of the same name, is one of the most outstanding properties in the district. This building, large and with a sober air, was ordered to be built by Phillip V in 1717 to house the Troops of the Royal Guard. The project was entrusted to Pedro de Ribera. After its restoration it was turned into the headquarters of the Newspaper Library, the City Archive, Central Public Library and Municipal Museum of Contemporary Art.

Very close by is one of the most welcoming and pleasant squares in Madrid, Plaza de las Comendadoras. Of note here is the convent of the Comendadoras de Santiago el Mayor, work of the architects Manuel and José del Olmo. Close to this area, in a small late-19th century palace is the interesting Cerralbo Museum. Its collection contains sculptures, archaeological objects, ornaments from the different branches of decorative arts and an endless list of objects that belonged to the Cerralbo family.

From Calle San Bernardo begins the area known as "Malasaña", the centre of which is Plaza del Dos de Mayo, overlooked by the monument to Daoiz and Velarde, heroes of the uprising against the French troops. Malasaña has been, since the return of democracy, one of the city's centres of counter-culture and nightlife. It is also in this area where there are such notable churches as the church of Nuestra Señora de Montserrat, in Calle San Bernardo; or the church of San Antonio de los Alemanes, en Corredera Baja de San Pablo.

Calle Fuencarral is the main commercial street in the district and the border that separates the districts of Maravillas and Chueca. Some of the best shops in Madrid with the latest trends, especially in fashion, are to be found

Plaza de Guardia de Corps (above). ▲
Jet market in the Plaza de las Comendadoras (below).
Plaza de las Comendadoras (above). ▶
Plaza del Dos de Mayo (below).

here. In the same street one can visit the History Museum (formerly the Municipal Museum), established in a spectacular Baroque building designed by Pedro de Ribera.

The Chueca district

Plaza de Chueca and Calle de Hortaleza are the two points of reference around which the Chueca district takes shape. This pleasant area has become really lively in recent years after being adopted by the gay community. On its streets traditional shops coexist with fashion shops, ambient bars and restaurants and specialised shops oriented towards the gay public.

At the end of Calle de Hortaleza, on the corner with Mejía Lequerica, we can appreciate a lovely example of early-20th century architecture. It is the Casa de los Lagartos. The name comes from the original lizards that support the cornice and closure of the flat roof.

In the nearby Calle de Fernando VI is one of the rare Modernist traces to be found in Madrid. It is the Palacio de Longoria, current headquarters of the SGAE (Society of Authors' Rights). This beautiful building was erected in 1903 by José Grases Riera. Its most outstanding elements are the large cylindrical tower of the corner and the profuse decoration with plant motifs on the façade.

Further on, in Calle Bárbara de Braganza, two massive examples of Baroque from the Bourbon period attract out attention: the church of the Salesas Reales, which is notable, above all, for the beautiful decoration of its main façade: and the Palacio de Justicia, current headquarters of the High Court. Both properties formed part of the old monastery of the Visitación, built in 1748 by the architects Francisco Carlier and Francisco Moradillo. In 1870, during the Revolutionary Sexennium, the church and the convent were secularized, and the latter was converted into the Palacio de Justicia. In 1924 it was completely reformed by Joaquín Rojí after a devastating fire.

Plaza de Chueca (above). ▲
Casa de los Lagartos. Detail (below).
Palacio de Longoria (above). ▶
Church of the Salesas Reales (below).

Parks where the city rests

There are times when one feels the need to escape from the coming and going, hustle and bustle and frenetic pace of the big city. This is when there is nothing better than hiding away in one of the green spaces that are distributed all around the city. Madrid has an extension of parks and gardens of more than 33 kilometers, as well as the 248,000 trees that adorn its streets and squares. Superb parks, such as the Retiro or the Parque del Oeste; gardens full of history, such as the Botanical Gardens or the palatial Sabatini Gardens and the Campo del Moro; also less-known corners such as the El Capricho park or the Fuente del Berro park. All of them are places for relaxing, strolling around and for letting the senses enjoy the natural richness and diversity of the city.

Parque del Retiro. Monument to Alfonso XII. ▶

The Parque del Retiro

The best option available in Madrid to momentarily escape from the rigours and frenzy of the city centre is, without doubt, the Parque del Retiro. It occupies an enormous area between Calle Alfonso XII, Calle Alcalá, Calle Menéndez Pelayo and Calle Poeta Esteban Villegas. The Retiro is the most important and emblematic green space in Madrid, the city's park par excellence. It is a spot of great beauty, and is frequented every day by locals and visitors alike who are in search of a breather. The Retiro has its own rhythm and particular idiosyncrasy. Strolling along its paths one can come across all sorts of characters: musicians from every corner of the globe, mime artists, storytellers, jugglers and street artists, fortune tellers and palmists, athletes... Without leaving the park one can undertake activities as diverse as tai-chi, rowing in the lake, visiting excellent exhibitions or, simply, sitting down and watching the world go by and enjoying a good read.

The history of the Retiro dates back to 1630, when the Count-Duke of Olivares decided to create a recreational residence for the sovereigns in an area close to the

Parque del Retiro. Lake (above). ▲
Statue of the Fallen Angel by the sculptor Ricardo Bellver (below).
Detail of a fountain in the lake. ▶

monastery of the Jerónimos. The works on the Real Sitio del Buen Retiro were carried out from 1632 to 1640 under the direction of Alonso de Carbonell. The result was a large palace surrounded by an extensive gardened area. Unfortunately, during the War of Independence (1808-1814) most of the palace and the gardens were destroyed after being used as a fort by the Napoleonic troops. Of the whole complex, only the Casón del Buen Retiro, the old Ballroom and the Kingdom Hall were conserved. Both buildings currently belong to the Prado Museum. During the kingdom of Ferdinand VII the partial reconstruction of the garden began, being completed around 1841. In 1868 the Parque del Retiro finally became municipal property.

There are lots of monuments and corners of great interest in the park. The lake, overlooked by an imposing monument to Alfonso XII, must be the most typical image of the Retiro. The monument is the work of the Catalan architect José Grasés Riera. The setting is made up of a large colonnade surrounding the equestrian statue of the monarch and a stairway that drops to the water adorned with stone lions and bronze allegories. It was opened in 1923 and some of the best sculptors of the time worked together on it. The most important contribution was the equestrian statue made by Mariano Benlliure. Among the fountains that adorn the Retiro we could highlight that of the Alcachofa (1781-1782), by the sculptors Alfonso Vergaz and Antonio Primo following a design by Ventura Rodríguez; and that of the Galápagos (1832), made by the architect José María Mariátegui and the sculptor José Tomás. Other spots with a singular charm are the Cecilio Rodríguez gardens and the Rosaleda. Among the many trees an example of Mexican cypress stands out as being the oldest tree in the park, and probably in the whole city. It comes from Mexico and was planted in 1633.

The statue of the Fallen Angel is perhaps the most famous and unique of those that adorn the Madrid park. It is located in the Paseo del Duque de Fernán Núñez, and is the only one in the world dedicated to the devil. It was produced in bronze by the sculptor Ricardo Bellver in 1874, and placed in its current position in 1885. It represents Lucifer expelled from paradise and with a snake coiled round him.

Finally, there are two magnificent buildings from the late-19th century by Ricardo Velázquez Bosco: The Palacio de Cristal, originally conceived as a greenhouse; and the

Crystal Palace in the Parque del Retiro. ▶

Palacio de Velázquez, built as the main pavilion for the National Mining Exhibition. Both now depend on the Reina Sofía National Museum and regularly house temporary exhibitions of contemporary art.

Parque del Oeste

The Parque del Oeste, one of the few English-style parks in the city, was designed by Cecilio Rodríguez in 1899. It occupies a surface area of 98 hectares made up of a large slope that goes from Calle del Pintor Rosales as far as the bank of the Manzanares. During the Civil, War it was the setting of tragic conflicts that left it seriously damaged. It had to be rebuilt by Cecilio Rodríguez himself after the struggle. With its large tree-filled meadows and steep slopes, it is undoubtedly one of the most beautiful parks in Madrid. In the lower part is one of the most charm-filled corners of the whole park, the Rosaleda, which has a wonderful collection of roses. Where Calle Marqués de Urquijo and Calle Pintor Rosales meet is the Cable Car that runs between the park and Casa de Campo.

The Parque del Oeste and the neighbouring Temple of Debod are perhaps the best spots in the whole city for taking in the famous Madrid sunsets.

Parque del Oeste. Temple of Debod (above). ▲
Cable car between Parque del Oeste and the Casa de Campo (below).
Rose garden in the Parque del Oeste. ▶

The temple of Debod is between the Parque del Oeste and Plaza de España. It is the oldest monument in Madrid and one of the most surprising in the entire city. The origin of the temple dates back to the 2nd century BC, was built by King Adikhalmani (Sudan) in honour of the gods Amon and Isis. It was originally located on the banks of the Nile, and was moved to make room for the Aswan Dam. In 1968 the Egyptian Government gave the temple to the Spanish Government. The monument was taken apart and packaged to be finally rebuilt in Madrid on the land of the old Montaña Military base, destroyed during the Civil War. The Temple of Debod is one of the most beautiful and unusual signs of identity of Madrid.

It is well worth visiting the popular hermitage of San Antonio de la Florida, located alongside the river, very close to the edge of the Parque del Oeste. Inside it houses a big surprise, some marvellous frescos painted by Francisco de Goya in 1798.

The Royal Botanical Gardens

Located at the start of Paseo del Prado, the Royal Botanical Gardens is one of the most charming and pleasant corners of the city. It is a veritable living museum where one can see an enormous variety of trees and plants from all over the world. Strolling along its paths is an instructive experience and a delight for the senses. The institution was founded in 1755, and in 1781 was moved to its current position. Charles III, within his enlightened programmes, wanted to place three large scientific institutions, the Natural History Museum (currently the main centre of the Prado Museum), the Astronomical Observatory and the Royal Botanical Gardens, in this part of the city. It was designed by Juan de Villanueva from a previous project by Sabatini.

After decades of abandon, the Botanical Gardens were restored between 1980 and 1981, giving it back their original appearance and splendour. It takes of nine hectares distributed on three staggered terraces. It contains approximately 5,000 different species of trees and plants. One of the most interesting points is the greenhouse devoted to the flora of tropical, temperate and desert climates.

Royal Botanical Garden. ▶

Other Parks

There are many other parks and gardens of the Massot varied styles in Madrid. Alongside the Palacio Real is, for example, the Sabatini Gardens and the Campo del Moro. The Parque de la Casa de Campo, recently closed to traffic, in the best of the city, with its 1,800 hectares is one of the big green spaces of the city. Inside the park is the Zoo and Amusement Park. The Parque de El Capricho, in Alameda de Osuna, is without doubt one of the most romantic and charming green spaces of the city. The Fuente del Berro, very close to Torre España, at the end of Calle Jorge Juan, is another spot with a singular charm. On the final section of Calle de Alcalá, level with the Suanzes metro station, is what is called Quinta de los Molinos, a beautiful and quiet park rather removed from the city centre, which is probably where its special charm comes from. Finally, we should mention the Juan Carlos I park, in an area close to the airport, alongside the IFEMA trade fair centre. It was opened in 1992 and houses, among other things, a municipal golf course. In summer it also hosts shows that combine light, water and sound.

Casa de Campo (above). ▲
Parque El Capricho (below).
Parque del Manzanares (above). ▶
Quinta de los Molinos (below).

The Community of Madrid

Beyond the numerous delights and attractions that the city of Madrid offers the visitor, in the Community of Madrid region there are other towns whose attractions should not be missed. A few kilometres from the capital and perfectly connected there are places as outstanding as the Real Sitio de San Lorenzo de El Escorial, the grand work of Phillip II turned into the political centre of his empire. Also linked to the Spanish monarchy is the history of the town of Aranjuez, with its magnificent palace and delicate gardens. Alcalá de Henares is one of the most important cities in the history of Spanish culture. It is no coincidence that it is the birthplace of Miguel de Cervantes, Cardinal Cisneros and Manuel Azaña. It is also the home of the Complutense University, the *Polyglot Bible* and the first *Castilian Gramática.* Finally, Chinchón provides one of the most delightful aspects of the whole region, featuring its Plaza Mayor and its characteristic lintelled galleries, the origin of which dates back to the Middle Ages.

Monastery of San Lorenzo de El Escorial. ▸

Monastery of San Lorenzo de El Escorial

The Real Sitio de San Lorenzo de El Escorial is some 45 kilometres northwest of Madrid. The monumental complex,
declared a World Heritage Site in 1984, was the grand work
of Phillip II, the political centre of his empire. The works
began in 1563 under the direction of Juan Bautista de Toledo.
After his death he was succeeded by his pupil Juan de
Herrera, which he completed in 1584. Herrera left a deep
impression on the complex. The final result is an enormous
parallelogram measuring 207 m by 161 m, crowned by a
tower in each of the tour angles. The main façade is made of
three doorways. The central one is the largest, in Doric style in
its lower section and Ionic in the upper section. It is crowned
by a low pediment on which are represented the coat of arms
of Phillip Felipe II and the image of Saint Lawrence Martyr
alongside to grilles, as a reminder of how the saint was mar-
tyred. El Escorial impresses the visitor due to its colossal size
and its solemn, sober and serious air.

General view (above). ▲
View from the library (below).
Courtyard of the Evangelists. ▶

For the decoration of the complex they were able to count on some of the best silversmiths and goldsmiths, painters and sculptors in Europe. Inside one can admire magnificent works of art, frescos by Lucas Jordán and Cambiasso, canvases by Velasquez, Goya, Titian or Bosch, and excellent sculptures, among which we should mention the spectacular *Christ* by Benvenuto Cellini.

The basilica, which is reached by crossing the Patio de Reyes, is the heart of the precinct. It has a Greek cross ground plan and comprises three naves, and features a large dome of 92 metres. The main chapel represents the magnitude of the project to perfection. Its magnificent altarpiece was designed by Juan de Herrera, with sculptures in bronze by Leoni father and son, and marbles by Juan Bautista Comane and Pedro Castello. The Kings' Pantheon is another of the more important spaces. Inside it houses the sepulchres of all the kings and queens of Hapsburg and Bourbon, except for Phillip V and Ferdinand VI, as well as the royal consorts who were the monarchs' mothers and fathers.

Library. ▲

General view from the monastery. ▶

Aranjuez

The history of this lovely town some 50 kilometres to the south of Madrid has been linked with the Crown since the times of the Catholic Monarchs. Its closeness to the capital, the mild climate and the abundance of game ensured that Aranjuez immediately became one of the favourite recreation spots of the Spanish monarchy.

The Palacio Real and its famous gardens, on the banks of the River Tajo, are the town's main attraction. In 1561, Phillip II ordered the construction of this luxurious building. The works were initially under the direction of Juan Bautista de Toledo and Juan de Herrera, also architects of El Escorial. The completion of the project was delayed for more than two centuries. The main façade was produced by Giacomo Bonavia during the reign of Ferdinand VII, and the two side façades and the chapel are the work of Sabatini, by then in the time of Charles III. The interior decoration is rich and diverse, in accordance with the tastes of the different monarchs. One can see valuable items of furniture of different styles and periods. Some of the most outstanding rooms are the Porcelain Museum and the Hall of Mirrors.

Aranjuez. Palacio Real (above). ▲
Palacio Real. Main façade (below).
Aranjuez Gardens: Fountain of Hércules (above). ▶
Príncipe Garden (below).

Perhaps the most interesting point is the lovely gardens that surround the palace, on the banks of the River Tajo. The Jardín del Príncipe, Jardín de la Isla and Jardín del Parterre, each with its own individual style, provide the visitor with a fabulous show for the senses. In 2001 UNESCO declared Aranjuez as a World Heritage Site.

Alcalá de Henares

The first impression one gets of this town 34 kilometres from Madrid may be deceptive. At first sight it may seem like just another dormitory city surrounding any large city. One must go into its beautiful old quarter in order to discover its historical, artistic and cultural history. Alcalá de Henares has had a key role in the cultural history of Spain. In 1547 Miguel de Cervantes Saavedra was born here, author of *Don Quixote*, one of the masterpieces of universal literature. It is also the birthplace of the Archpriest of Hita, Cardinal Cisneros and Manuel Azaña. Here is where the Complutense University arose, the *Polyglot Bible* and the first Castilian *Gramática*. This valuable legacy is perfectly in line with the declaration in 1998 as a World Heritage Site.

University of Alcalá de Henares (above). ▲
Alcalá de Henares. Statue of Cervantes (below).
University courtyard. ▶

The life of this city has been very closely linked to the Complutense University, founded by Cardinal Cisneros in 1499. This centre soon acquired great prestige throughout Europe. Among many others, its classrooms were attended by a large section of key figures from the Golden Century. The old university was made up of a major college, the college of San Ildefonso, and a series of smaller colleges dependent on it. The oldest building of the complex is the chapel of San Ildefonso, built in 1510. In its interior one can admire an exceptional Mudejar coffered ceiling, and the beautiful sepulchre of Cardinal Cisneros, carved in Carrara marble by Domenico Fancelli and Bartolomé Ordóñez.

As well as the University it is well worth visiting other points of great interest spread around the old quarter. Among the most outstanding we could mention the Cervantes House-Museum, the monastery of the Bernardas, the Palacio de Laredo, the Master Cathedral, the Archbishopric Palace and the Archaeological Museum.

Walls of Alcalá de Henares. ▲

Alcalá de Henares. General view. ▸

Chinchón

Chinchón is 47 kilometres southeast of Madrid. It is one of the most picturesque and most charm-filled towns in the region. The Plaza Mayor, of medieval origin, is an example of popular architecture of singular beauty and one of the main signs of identity of the town. It has an irregular structure, and is made up of a series of three-storey buildings with lintelled galleries. The 234 wooden balconies that face the square complete its characteristic image. It is the town's nerve centre, witness to its entire history. Over the centuries it has been the setting for political and religious, royal festivals, theatre and celebrations, proclamations, eucharistic plays and executions.

Strolling around the old quarter of Chinchón one can visit many other important spots. Some of the most outstanding are the Clock Towers, the remains of the castle of the Counts, the hermitages of San Antón, San Roque and that of Nuestra Señora de la Misericordia, and the convents of San Agustín (currently Parador de Turismo hotel) and the convent of the Clarisas. Special mention should be made of the church of Nuestra Señora de la Asunción (15th century), the interior of which shows the painting of the *Assumption of the Virgin* painted by Goya.

Plaza Mayor of Chinchón (above). ▲
Chinchón. Ethnological Museum (below).
Plaza Mayor of Chinchón. ▶

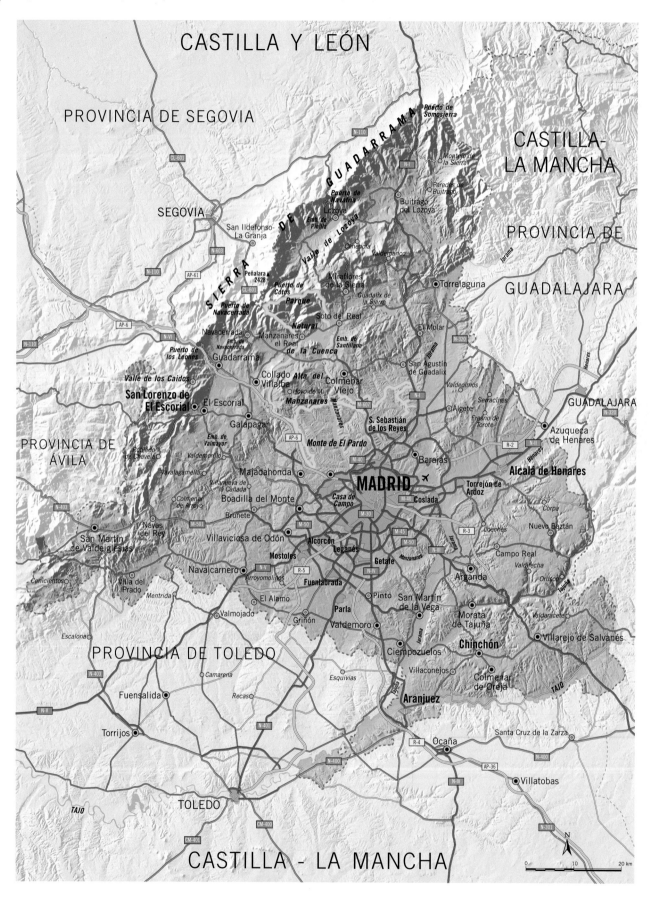